Toronto Blue
the Bat Boy for the Blue Jays

Written and Illustrated

By

Cameron Silver

Black Mesa Publishing

Florida

Dedicated to Blue Jays fans everywhere!

If I was the Bat Boy for the Toronto Blue Jays, I would work at Rogers Centre and live in Canada.

I would gather the baseball equipment before the game starts...

collect the bats after a player gets a hit...

clean the players' cleats...

and wash and clean the players' batting helmets.

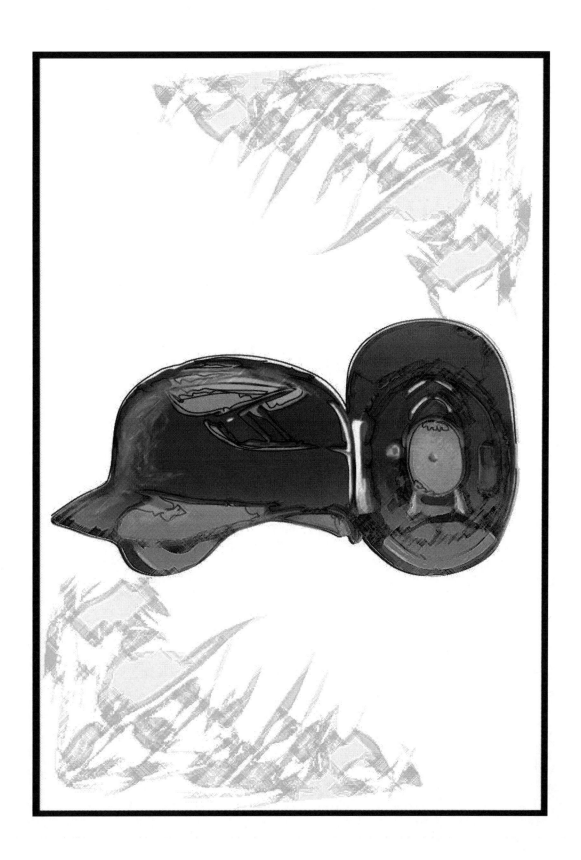

If I was the Blue Jays Bat Boy, I would have taken batting practice with Tony Fernandez and George Bell.

I would have played catch
with Roberto Alomar
and
John Olerud.

If I was the Bat Boy for the Blue Jays, I would have seen them win the

1993 World Series after

Joe Carter's series ending home run.

I would have helped

Dave Steib,

Roy Halladay and

Phil Niekro

warm up their pitching arms.

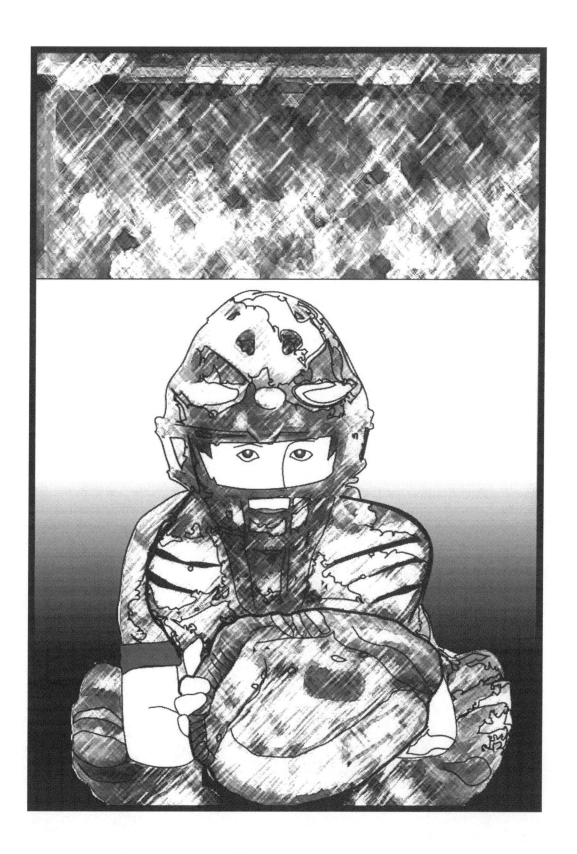

I would listen to the Manager call out plays from the dugout.

If I was the Blue Jays
Bat Boy, I'd be a winner!

If I was the Blue Jays Bat Boy, I'd watch Toronto win the

World Series!!!!

(Two and counting!!!)

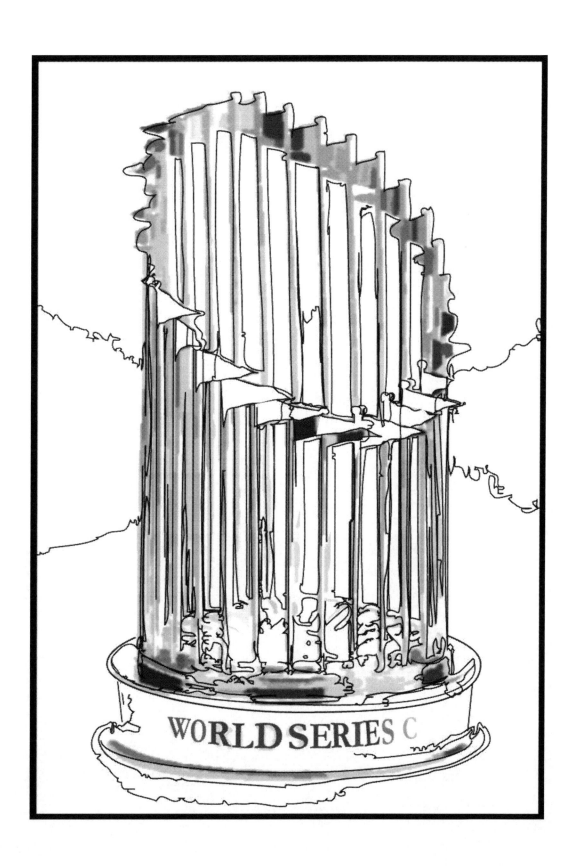

Manufactured by Amazon.ca
Bolton, ON

53317341R00017